Interpreting Our Dreams

by Mrs. Prisco's fifth-grade class

Table of Contents

The Assignment

The students in Mrs. Prisco's fifth-grade class recently completed a unit on sleep and dreams. For the final assignment in the unit, the students had to compile a dream journal and then give a presentation to the class. Every morning from Tuesday to Thursday, the students wrote down their dreams upon waking. They **pondered** what the dreams meant, and used what they had learned to interpret them. Then, on Friday, they each presented their overall analysis. Combined, the journal and the presentation counted as their science midterm examination.

The following are three of the students' journals.

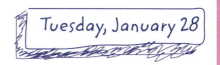

The Dream Journal
of Alyssa M. Silver

Dearest Dream Journal,

I am excited to report that I just had a dream to write about! But I'm confused by what it means.

When the dream began, I was standing in an unfamiliar locker room wearing a purple and white basketball uniform, and all around me were girls my age in the same **attire**. We sat listening to our coach prepping us for the second half.

"It's time to get serious, girls!" Coach said. "This is the most important game of our season, so we need to get out there and turn things around!"

Out on the court, I shot the ball over and over again, and all my teammates cheered me on, high-fiving me after every basket. I was on fire! Yet somehow, when I looked up at the scoreboard, it said BEARS: 48 / AWAY: 52. We were still losing despite all of the points I had just scored.

With seconds left, I scored again. Then the other team got the ball and started down the court. I tried to run back to get on defense, but now I couldn't run. My legs felt heavy and I could barely lift them off the ground. It was as if I was running in deep water.

Finally, I struggled back to defend our basket. The other team shot the ball, but missed. The rebound fell right into my hands. I immediately began to dribble down the court, but again I was moving in the slowest of slow motion. What's weird was that I was the only one going slowly. Around me, my teammates were running at full speed and yelling, "Pass the ball." The crowd was jumping up and down and calling my name. "Alyssa! Alyssa! Alyssa!"

I felt so frustrated and really confused, but I kept dribbling in slow motion toward the other team's basket. When I managed to make it to the three-point line, I lifted my arms and prepared to shoot.

But then I couldn't move my arms. They were frozen in midair, like icicles pointing upward. I could wiggle my body and move my legs, but my arms would not budge and neither would my fingers. It was as if someone had glued the ball to my palms. My teammates looked at me **frantically**, but I just stood there, helpless and embarrassed.

Then the buzzer sounded, and we lost 50–52. If I had only taken the shot, and made it, we would have won.

Immediately, the other team started celebrating, and I woke up.

Based on what we learned in class, this dream would clearly be considered an anxiety dream. Anxiety is a strong feeling of uneasiness and fear. The confusing part, though, is what the anxiety is about. I don't play on a basketball team—I've only played in gym class at school. And none of the girls or the coach looked like anyone I know. I do play lacrosse in a recreation league, but that doesn't start until the end of March, so I don't think it's about that.

There must be some deeper anxiety that the dream is pulling out. Dr. Sigmund Freud, the father of **psychoanalysis**, would likely **theorize** that something in my **unconscious** mind is bothering me. I guess I will have to think more about it and see what happens tomorrow night.

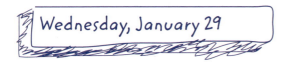

Dearest Dream Journal,

Last night I had another dream about being unable to do something. This time I was at school, back in my third-grade class with Mrs. Anderson. I had the distinct feeling that I didn't belong in that classroom. My dreaming self seemed to know that something was wrong. In my dream, I even thought to myself, *Wait, I'm in fifth grade now! Did I get sent back for some reason? Why am I here?*

Suddenly, a loud screeching filled the room as Mrs. Anderson scraped her chalk across the board. The words POP QUIZ extended forward from the board like words in a 3-D movie. She poked the words with her chalk and they **fizzled** like a deflated balloon.

I wondered what the quiz would be about, but when I looked down at the paper, all I saw was **gibberish**. There were letters in word-sized chunks, but none of them looked like any words I had ever seen before.

I had an intense feeling of nervousness. I raised my hand to see if the teacher would help me, but she would not look in my direction. Then I opened my mouth to say, "Mrs. Anderson, I don't understand this," but nothing came out. I could feel my lips moving, but I couldn't hear my own voice, and it was obvious that no one else could either.

Looking around, I saw that everyone else was already writing on their papers, and quickly. Their pencil-gripping hands dashed across the papers as if in a race.

The other students in the class were a strange assortment. They were not my classmates from third grade or even my classmates from fifth grade. I saw a teammate from my lacrosse team who doesn't even go to my school. My best friend from my old neighborhood was there—and she still looked like she was five! My cousin was sitting next to me—and he lives in California! It was all so weird.

"Two more minutes!" Mrs. Anderson called out.

Two more minutes! But she just handed out the quiz! And I can't even read what this says!

"Mrs. Anderson, there's something wrong with my paper," I said, handing it to her.

"I'm not sure what you mean, Alyssa. It looks the same as everyone else's. Right there, at the top, it says *Charlotte's Web*."

I couldn't understand why she would make such a ridiculous claim. Nothing on my paper looked like *Charlotte's Web*. Not even one of those letters was there. I could definitely take a quiz about that book. I had read it so many times, I practically had it memorized.

"Time's up!" Mrs. Anderson called out.

I looked down at my paper and all of a sudden real words started to appear. *This can't be!* I thought. *How could I have been so wrong?*

Then ever so slowly, spider webs started to appear in the corners of the classroom. Then they got larger. Then there were webs from the ceiling to my desk!

Out of the corner of my eye, I saw a dark shape moving closer to me. It came closer and closer and finally I could make out what it was—a giant, hairy spider with creepy eyes. Then it moved one of its eight hairy legs toward me and I screamed at the top of my lungs.

I don't know if I screamed in real life, but either the sound of my own screams or the sight of that spider woke me right up. I sat straight up in my bed and thought I could still hear my screams, but it was actually my alarm clock. It was time to get up for school. I don't think I've ever been so happy to wake up!

This dream is something like the other one I had, but I'm still not sure what's causing them, or my anxiety. Why would I be worried about being able to read when reading is one of my favorite things to do? I even won an award for having read the most books over the summer. And why would I be nervous about a pop quiz? Unlike Mrs. Anderson, Mrs. Prisco always gives us fair warning for quizzes.

The **logical** answer would be that I'm worried about my midterm exams, but I've already studied for them and feel totally prepared. It has to be something else; but what, I don't know.

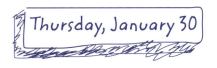

Dearest Dream Journal,

Finally, my dream last night provided me with the missing piece for my analysis.

In the dream, I was standing on a stage in a crowded auditorium. In front of the stage, there was a table with huge books piled high atop it. Several robed judges with colonial wigs sat at the table and looked sternly at me and the other students behind me onstage.

That's when I noticed that I didn't have any shoes on. What was I doing barefoot on a stage in front of other people? This fact was really bothering me and it was all I could think about. I looked behind me and under the podium. My *shoes have to be here somewhere,* I thought.

"Miss Silver! Miss Silver! Did you hear me?" one of the judges called out. "Your word is *deciduous.*"

I realized I must be in a spelling bee.

The pounding of my heart echoed in my ears, and my stomach did somersaults. My palms felt sweaty and my face flushed. This chain of physical responses happened every time I had to speak in front of a group of people.

Okay, I told myself, *just breathe.* I let out a long, slow breath and watched it float out over the crowd as a white, puffy cloud.

I knew how to spell that word.

"*Deciduous.* D-E-C-I-D . . . ," I started, and then my brain just stopped. It halted so suddenly, that my head even lurched forward with the force of it.

"Uh . . . Uh . . . I'm sorry," I stammered as I turned and ran off the stage.

I just kept running and running, out of the auditorium, down the hall, and through the front door into a bright, blinding light.

My eyes shot open and I sat up in my bed.

It suddenly all made sense. I knew what my dreams had been about!

Samantha Tucker's Dream Journal

Hey, Dream Journal,

I think I will call you D.J. for short. My friends and I all call each other by our nicknames. Mine's Sam, as I'm sure you might have guessed.

I think this assignment could be fun because I usually have pretty cool dreams. In my dreams, I often do things I really want to do someday, like zip-lining through a rain forest in Costa Rica or bungee jumping into the Grand Canyon.

Sometimes I'm flying. I have had a **recurring** dream where I'm holding a magic board out in front of me like you do with a kickboard in a pool. Then I take off into the air. The funny part is that I always wake up holding on to my pillow!

Last night, though, my dream wasn't that adventurous. I was running, but I wasn't in a competition, or even running just for fun. Instead, I was being chased by someone. Even though I couldn't see the person chasing me at first, I knew he or she was there.

Sprinting through a crowded city street, I pushed my way through the tightly packed bodies, weaving in and out amongst them. I turned a corner and paused to catch my breath, but then I sensed the presence of my predator and took off again.

I need to get off the street and hide, I thought. So I ducked into what seemed like the world's largest department store. I saw one of those circular racks filled with clothes and crawled into the center. I waited there holding my breath until I saw feet run by. Then I waited a minute or so more and dashed back out through the store the same way I came in. I thought I had lost the mystery person, when all of a sudden I heard the sound of heavy footsteps behind me. Yipes! I was off and running again.

My heart raced as my feet pounded the pavement and I leaped over a fallen garbage pail and rolled across the hood of a parked car. If only I wasn't being chased, I would have been enjoying this city-street obstacle course.

Trying to trick my pursuer, I turned left around a corner and then left again. With each turn, I sensed that the figure was falling farther back and I was convinced that I was going to get away. But then there she was, standing right in front of me.

Immediately I knew it was the person chasing me. She stood in my path wearing a red, hooded robe, like the ones boxers wear before a match. The robe blocked her face so I couldn't see the details of her features. I spun around to head back the other way and instantly she was in front of me again. It wasn't a duplicate or a twin, but the same girl who had relocated herself somehow.

I realized there was no escaping, so I walked toward her to get a better look at who I was up against. And then I saw that her face was my own!

I slowly came awake with this **realization** fresh in my mind. I don't need to question what this dream means. I was running away from myself.

Hey, D.J.,

I don't have much time to write to you today because I have to get ready for wrestling team tryouts, but my dream was very short anyway.

At first, I was walking along a tightrope over Niagara Falls like that daredevil guy I saw on TV. I was feeling pretty steady, slowly but surely putting one foot directly in front of the other. I heard the sound of wind picking up and my heart started to race. A gust of wind blew across my body, and I wobbled a little, but I kept moving forward. Then an even larger gust of wind blew me and I lost balance. I teetered and fell off the rope. What was so unnerving was that I didn't splash into the falls or hit the water below. I just kept falling through the air as if the Earth's surface was miles away.

So, down and down I went, tumbling end over end. It could have been **exhilarating**, but I was scared senseless not knowing when I would hit the water, or even if I *would* hit water. Maybe I would hit solid ground instead.

I could hear my own screams as if they were coming from outside of my body, and they sounded like one long continuous "AAAAAAAAHHHHHHHH!"

Then the next thing I knew, I found myself waking up on the floor next to the bed.

I've never fallen before in a dream, but I know it was one of the common dreams we talked about in class. Mrs. Prisco said that most people interpret falling dreams as a feeling of being out of control, and that makes total sense for my dream.

It also makes sense in terms of what I'm about to do. Tryouts for the wrestling team are today, and I finally had the courage yesterday to ask Coach Winters if I could try out. If I make it, I'll be the first girl to ever be on the team, but right now, everything feels completely out of my control.

Hey, D.J.,

Guess what? I MADE THE TEAM!

Sorry to shout, but I can't help it because I am so pumped up about being on the team! All of my worries were for nothing. My friends were there to cheer me on and they were super happy for me when I made it. They thought it was awesome how I showed the guys just how tough a girl can be.

Anyway, I guess I'm really supposed to be telling you about my dream from last night. It definitely relates to me making the team, so I wasn't totally off topic.

My dream last night was the best one of the week because I finally got to have fun doing something thrilling, like I usually do in my dreams.

16

I was standing in a wide open field on a beautiful sunny day and the air had that fresh smell of a light summer rain. I breathed in deeply to fill my nostrils with the scent.

Then suddenly I ran with my arms spread wide, jumped into the air, and started gliding. I wasn't holding on to anything and I wasn't the slightest bit scared. I wasn't even surprised by my own abilities. It was as if I had been flying my whole life.

I flew through the air over wide expanses of open desert, past the peaks of mountains, then down over the vast plains, and back up over tall skyscrapers. Without **exerting** any effort, I soared across the country and back again.

I have never felt so free before, in life or in my dreams. It was absolutely amazing!

My Dream Journal

by Mayur Patel

Hi, Dream Journal,

Are you ready to hear about a really bizarre dream? Because the dream I had last night was incredibly strange.

I was walking through a dense forest full of trees bright with crimson leaves, and I could hear a voice talking up ahead of me, but I didn't see anyone.

"Hello? Is anyone there?" I called out.

"Of course there is. I'm standing right in front of you!"

Startled, I jumped back and tumbled onto the ground. Then to my amazement, a glowing smile twinkled in front of me, and a long nose stretched back from it. Piece by piece, the sparkling, shadowy shape of a beautiful blue horse appeared until finally it looked like a solid form.

"What . . . uh . . . what are you? And better yet, how did you just appear like that?" I asked, hiding my fear with a stern tone.

"My boy, my boy," the creature replied, as I rose to my feet. "You must learn not to ask so many questions. Your mouth will do you no good here, I'm afraid. To learn about this special place, you must use your ears and your eyes."

Then he reared back on his hind legs and came back down, slamming his hooves to the ground and charging at me. But instead of colliding into me, his ghostly presence passed right through, coating my clothing with shimmering blue glitter.

The only thing I felt was a sense of warm air passing over my skin. But then my mouth started to come together and my lips sealed shut, tight against my face. No matter how hard I tried, I couldn't open them. I felt my eyes bulge from their sockets and my ears grow twice their size.

What on Earth did that creature do to me?

I turned to run out of the forest and suddenly the grass became a wooden plank, and I ran right onto a ship. Only it wasn't a regular-sized ship and I had to bend my body practically in half to fit inside the ridiculously small cabin.

Standing at the steering wheel of the ship was a large white rabbit that looked like a holiday display at the mall. The rabbit wasn't unfriendly, but it was very serious, as if captaining this ship was incredibly important. It was odd to see a big, furry rabbit acting so intense and it made me feel nervous.

"Welcome aboard, Mayur," the large rabbit said with a salute. "We've been waiting for you."

"How are you talking?" I asked the rabbit.

"How are you talking?" he asked me right back. "It seems that talking is just talking, we all do it pretty much the same way. But perhaps what you need to do is listen."

Suddenly a huge wave came across the bow of the boat. I felt the water hit my face and suddenly I was awake in my bed. Instead of water, a beam of sunlight was on my face.

Well, journal, I'm not really sure what to say about this dream. The only thing I can think of is that the dream was telling me I should listen more. My mom is always telling me to do that.

It was certainly weirder than any other dream I have ever had, and I've had some pretty strange ones. I have also learned in class that sometimes dreams are affected by the last thing you saw on TV or the last thing you ate. Maybe it was caused by those spicy jalapeños I had in my taco for dinner.

Please-Touch Museum

Hi, Dream Journal,

Last night, there weren't any horses or huge rabbits magically appearing in my dream, but toys did come to life and try to steal my brain power. Yes, it was as weird as it sounds.

At the beginning of the dream, I was walking into the Please-Touch Museum. This was my favorite place to visit when I was a little kid, and my family still goes there a lot because my little twin sisters love it.

The museum was completely empty, but for some reason, I tiptoed as I entered and stopped to look up at the huge liberty torch melded from old toys. Every time we go to the museum nowadays, my parents always have to point out the favorite toys from their childhoods that are part of the statue.

Deciding to take advantage of my free rein of the museum, I ran around splashing water, banging rain-forest instruments, and spinning on the carousel. I was just about to run down the twisty ramp to the lower level, when I heard a loud voice yell "STOP HIM!"

I considered whether I should take off or just stay still, but my **hesitation** made that decision for me.

I felt a coarse material being wrapped around my legs. I looked down to see a small brown figure with bumpy eyes and big red lips tying a rope. Then everything went black.

The next thing I knew, I was on a long bench in the entrance hall of the museum with my arms and legs tied down and some kind of electrical equipment attached to my head. Toys of all kinds surrounded me and stood on top of my body. There were marching soldiers, cooing baby dolls, stuffed bears, a pull-along puppy, and a talking telephone. There were even plastic fruits and vegetables, wooden blocks, and rubber balls—all with moving eyes and small **appendages**.

"What are you doing to me?" I asked them.

"Touching you, of course; this is the *Please-Touch* Museum, isn't it?" said a banana. "Day after day, little grimy hands touch us nonstop, and occasionally, when some poor soul wanders in here after dark, we get to have our turn."

"But how are you talking and moving? And why do you and the other plastic fruits have eyes and limbs?" I asked.

"That's what this is for," the potato said, tapping the machine attached to my head. "We also suck out all your brain power because that's how we keep ourselves going."

"Good luck trying to get my brain power!" I shouted. "I'm a big kid and you're just a bunch of little toys."

I thrashed my body back and forth, and some of the toys fell to the ground, but with each one that fell, more climbed back up. They called in reinforcements, and soon I was drowning under the weight of them.

I woke up, tossing and turning inside my twisted sheets.

I glanced over at the toys on my bookcase and shuddered in fright. Why would I dream of being tortured by toys? Did I secretly feel guilty for shoving my sisters' dolls out of my way yesterday? Maybe I should be more careful with them from now on.

Hi, Dream Journal,

So, I have another strange dream to tell you about. In this one, I was living on Mars and my home was one of many in a neighborhood of identical houses. But aside from the red dust covering the ground, you would never know the houses were on Mars because the neighborhood was within walking distance of an ocean and there were lush trees everywhere.

In the dream, I was sitting in my house watching a movie about aliens living on planet Earth. To a resident of Mars, these curious aliens, called humans in their native language, seemed peculiar in every way.

Halfway through the film, the screen turned bright green and a deafening static noise blared. WARNING! The message read: *Hurricane ZERK-Q10 has been sighted and is about to hit land near Crater Falls.*

Outside of my house, the wind whipped through the trees, and I could hear branches cracking and crashing to the ground. And then without any warning, a tremendous rush of water poured down the street and through the door, knocking me off my feet.

Quickly, water collected in the small hut, pushing everything around inside. Within minutes, the water was up to my waist, and then just as quickly, it receded.

The hut was an absolute mess. Everything was knocked over haphazardly and every surface was covered with a nasty red mud.

Not knowing what to do next, I walked out of my house and down the street to assess everyone else's damage. I turned in a circle, dumbfounded by all the destruction around me. Then I kept turning around and around, spinning in dizzying circles . . . until I woke up.

For several minutes after waking, I just sat in my bed confused. I didn't know how the planet Mars and a hurricane could be connected, or how this dream related to the other two.

I grabbed for the glass of water on my nightstand and accidentally knocked over one of the books that sat there. I looked at the rest of the pile of books, and then instantly everything clicked.

Excerpts from the Presentations

Friday, January 31

On Friday, Alyssa, Samantha, and Mayur all presented their dream analyses to the class. The following are excerpts from their presentations:

Alyssa

All of my dreams could be classified as anxiety dreams. In each one, I attempted to do something but couldn't because my body or my brain **malfunctioned** in some way. At first I was confused about what was causing this anxiety, but after my dream on Wednesday night, it became very clear to me what I had been dreaming about all week. In that dream, I was terrified of performing before an audience in a spelling bee. My brain froze as I started to spell a word I knew, and I was so embarrassed that all I could do was run from the stage.

This showed me that the anxiety causing my dreams was about public speaking. Usually I don't feel nervous until right before a presentation, but this presentation must have been stirring up anxiety deep inside me. That anxiety came out in different forms through my dreams.

Anxiety About Oral Presentation		
unable to run or shoot a basketball and my team loses	unable to understand words on a pop quiz	brain freezes during spelling bee

Samantha

Even though I had very common dreams that a lot of people have—being chased, falling, and flying—they were specific to me and my situation.

You all know that I just made the wrestling team and that I am the first girl at our school to do so, but you might not know that I had a hard time deciding whether I should even try out. For weeks, I worried about what might happen because I didn't know how my friends and the boys on the team would react.

This helps explain why my first dream was about running away from myself. Rather than address my feelings, I was trying to run from them. Once I realized this, I decided to talk to Coach Winters and ask permission to try out. Getting past that gave me some relief. Though this was a relief, things were still out of my control, and later that night, I dreamed of falling from a great height. Finally the next day, I tried out and made the team and both my friends and the boys on the team were really cool about it. I was free from worry and free to follow my dream! And I experienced that freedom in my last dream, as I flew like a bird high up in the sky.

Being Chased	Falling	Flying
running away from feelings	feeling out of control	feeling relieved and free

Mayur

My dreams this week were definitely strange—there were magical creatures, and scary toys, and a hurricane on Mars. I was completely **stumped** as to how these things reflected the common symbols we learned about in our unit on dreams or how they could relate to my life.

And then yesterday morning, I saw the books on my nightstand. Every night before bed, I had been rereading from the books to prepare for our midterm. I had read from *Alice in Wonderland*, *The Black Stallion*, *Toys!*, *Discovering Mars*, and *Hurricanes!* Bits and pieces of what I had read had come alive in my dreams. I guess it was my brain's way of continuing to think about the books even after I had gone to sleep.

Glossary

appendages   (uh-PEN-dih-jez) *noun* arms and legs (page 24)

attire   (uh-TIRE) *noun* clothing (page 3)

exerting   (ig-ZER-ting) *verb* putting forth an effort (page 17)

exhilarating   (ig-ZIH-luh-ray-ting) *adjective* exciting; thrilling
(page 14)

fizzled   (FIH-zuld) verb made a hissing sound (page 6)

frantically   (FRAN-tik-lee) *adverb* with panic or fear (page 4)

gibberish   (JIH-buh-rish) *noun* nonsense; meaningless words
(page 6)

hesitation   (heh-zih-TAY-shun) *noun* act of waiting or pausing,
usually to think about something before doing it (page
23)

logical   (LAH-jih-kul) *adjective* making sense (page 8)

malfunctioned   (mal-FUNK-shund) *verb* stopped working
(page 28)

pondered   (PAHN-derd) *verb* thought about in depth (page 2)

psychoanalysis (sy-koh-uh-NA-lih-sis) *noun* a type of therapy where
the patient talks freely about his experiences, often
focusing on dreams and childhood (page 5)

realization   (ree-uh-lih-ZAY-shun) *noun* a conclusion made from
thinking about something (page 13)

recurring   (rih-KER-ing) *verb* happening over and over (page 11)

stumped   (STUMPT) *adjective* confused; puzzled about
(page 30)

theorize   (THEE-uh-rize) *verb* make a theory, or suggestion,
about (page 5)

unconscious   (un-KAHN-shus) *adjective* not part of one's awareness
(page 5)

Analyze the Text

Questions for Close Reading

Use facts and details from the text to support your answers to the following questions.

- Why does Alyssa refer to Sigmund Freud in her first journal entry? How does this relate to her final analysis about her dreams?

- In Alyssa's third journal entry, she says, "The pounding of my heart echoed in my ears, and my stomach did somersaults." What does this mean and why does she say this?

- How does Samantha feel about her falling dream? Cite specific details from her journal to support your response.

- What is Mayur's final interpretation of his strange dreams? Explain how each of his dreams relates to this theory.

Comprehension: Make Inferences

Good readers use clues from the text to make inferences about things that are not directly stated. For each of the students in the text, write a statement from one of their journal entries, and then explain an inference you can make from that statement.

People	Statement from Journal Entry	Inference
Alyssa		
Samantha		
Mayur		